Exploring History 1

Workbook

Moderated by
Dr. Christa Lohmann

Written by
Rolf J. Kröger
Dr. Deanna Nebert
Barbara Nerlich
Thomas Söhrnsen

westermann

Eine kommentierte Linkliste befindet sich unter:
www.westermann.de/gymnasium/geschichte.xtp

© 2008 Bildungshaus Schulbuchverlage
Westermann Schroedel Diesterweg Schöningh Winklers GmbH, Braunschweig
www.westermann.de

Das Werk und seine Teile sind urheberrechtlich geschützt. Jede Nutzung in anderen als den gesetzlich
zugelassenen Fällen bedarf der vorherigen schriftlichen Einwilligung des Verlages. Hinweis zu § 52 a
UrhG: Weder das Werk noch seine Teile dürfen ohne eine solche Einwilligung gescannt und in ein Netz-
werk eingestellt werden. Dies gilt auch für Intranets von Schulen und sonstigen Bildungseinrichtungen.
Auf verschiedenen Seiten dieses Buches befinden sich Verweise (Links) auf Internet-Adressen. Haftungs-
hinweis: Trotz sorgfältiger inhaltlicher Kontrolle wird die Haftung für die Inhalte der externen Seiten aus-
geschlossen. Für den Inhalt dieser externen Seiten sind ausschließlich deren Betreiber verantwortlich.
Sollten Sie bei dem angegebenen Inhalt des Anbieters dieser Seite auf kostenpflichtige, illegale oder
anstößige Inhalte treffen, so bedauern wir dies ausdrücklich und bitten Sie, uns umgehend per E-Mail
davon in Kenntnis zu setzen, damit beim Nachdruck der Verweis gelöscht wird.

Druck A[1] / Jahr 2008
Alle Drucke der Serie A sind im Unterricht parallel verwendbar.

Redaktion: Christoph Meyer, Dorle Bennöhr
Herstellung: Udo Sauter
Typografie: Thomas Schröder
Satz: pva, Druck und Medien-Dienstleistungen GmbH, Landau
Druck und Bindung: westermann druck GmbH, Braunschweig

ISBN 978-3-14-**11 1058**-6

1. Absolutism and Enlightenment 4

I. Principles of Absolutism 4
II. The Royal Puppet Player – Louis XIV 5
III. The Huguenots 6
IV. Mercantilism 7
V. The Image of the Monarch – Symbols of Power 8
VI. Louis's France – Revision 9
VII. A Great Leap 10
VIII. Frederick II, the Enlightened Monarch 11

2. The American Revolution 12

I. National Treasures 12
II. The Trail of Tears 14
III. The Course of American History – Revision 15

3. The French Revolution 16

I. The First Phase of the Revolution 16
II. The King's Flight 18
III. Was the Terror Necessary? 20
IV. The 16 Steps of the Revolution 21
V. Napoleon's Rise and Downfall 22
VI. Reforms in Prussia 23

4. Industrialization 24

I. Population Explosion 24
II. Revolution in Transport 25
III. Triumph of Electricity 26
IV. Living Conditions – Housing 27
V. Child Labour 28
VI. The Strike 30
VII. Social Security 32
VIII. Summary – From Cottage Industry to Factory Industry 33

5. The Struggle for Unity and Liberty 34

I. The Congress of Vienna and the Holy Alliance 34
II. Political Murder 35
III. The Frankfurt Parliament, 1848-49 36
IV. Debates in the Assembly 38

6. Imperial Germany 40

I. Proclamation of the German Empire, 1871 40
II. Differences in Voting in Germany and Prussia 42
III. The Socialist Law and the End of the Kulturkampf 44
IV. Women's Suffrage 46

7. New Imperialism and the Scramble for Africa 48

I. Personality: Emperor William II of Germany (1859-1941) 48
II. The "New Course" 50
III. German Colonialism: "Healing the Wounds of the Past" 52
IV. Africa Today 54

8. The First World War 56

I. 1914 – the Road to War 56
II. The Alliances of Europe in 1914 57
III. Analysing Propaganda 58
IV. Working with statistics 60
V. Revision 62

1. Absolutism and Enlightenment

I. Principles of Absolutism

M 1 Diagram of the Inside of the Royal Chapel at Versailles:

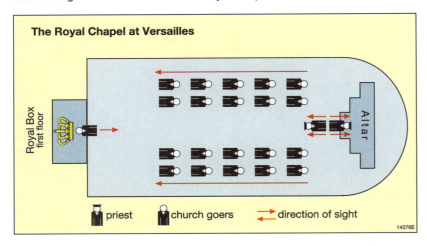

1. Explain what the seating order and the direction of sight show about the position of the king.

_____
_____
_____
_____

M 2 Bishop Bossuet was in charge of teaching the crown prince. In this article he tells him why France needs a monarchy.

"The whole world begins with the monarchical form of the state. Its foremost example can be found in the authority of the father in the family, i.e. in nature itself. People are all born as subjects, and through the authority of their fathers, which acquaints them with obedience, they are also used to the idea of having only one leader. Monarchy is the most permanent and therefore the strongest form of government. National union can never be better realized than under one king. The prince sees things from a higher point of view; we can be sure that he sees farther than we can; that is why we must obey him without complaint: complaining is as good as tending to revolt. Princes act as God's servants and governors on earth. It is through them that He governs. The king need never account for what he commanded. He cannot do good or suppress bad without his absolute power. The only way for his subject to protect himself against this supreme power is to maintain his complete innocence… Therefore, the subject who refuses to obey his prince must be sentenced to death as an enemy of human society. The prince incorporates the entire government in his own person; the will of the people is realized through him. The prince can correct himself, when he notices that he has done evil. The king's authority is subject to reason. Kings may use their power only for the common good of their countries.

Bossuet, Politics according to the Holy Writ.

2. Can you imagine living in a monarchy as it is described in Bossuet's text?

3. Compare your life to the lives of people at that time.

_____
_____
_____

| 1640 | 1655 | 1670 | 1685 | 1700 | 1715 | 1730 | 1745 | 1760 | 1775 | 1790 |

II. The Royal Puppet Player – Louis XIV

1. Label the 'puppets' Louis could play with.

2. Describe the cartoon in detail.

_____
_____
_____
_____

3. Explain the meaning of the inscription in the halo.

_____
_____
_____

4. Find out why nobility is missing.

_____
_____
_____

5

1. Absolutism and Enlightenment

III. The Huguenots

An earlier French king, Henry IV, had granted the Huguenots important rights and privileges in his Edict of Nantes in 1598. As a result, most of them remained loyal to the French crown. Some of them even served in the army, but nearly all contributed to the economy as they believed they should work hard and improve business as much as possible. A high percentage of the Huguenots were prominent in industry and trade. They were also dedicated craftsmen, skilled in pottery, silk and glass-making, as well as weavers, tailors, clockmakers, goldsmiths, hatters and wig-makers.

According to the idea of ONE RELIGION in France, Louis XIV first hoped the Huguenots would become Catholics. But after 1677, he suddenly determined to wipe out their religion.

M 1 **Edict of Fontainebleau**

In 1685 Louis cancelled the Edict of Nantes in a new Edict of Fontainebleau. Here are some excerpts from it:

"Clause 4. We command all ministers and priests of the Huguenots, who do not wish to become Catholics, to leave Our kingdom within fifteen days, without during that time preaching to their people, upon pain of being sent to the galleys.
Clause 7. We forbid private schools for the instruction of the children of the said Huguenots.
Clause 8. All children who may be born to Huguenots are to be baptised by Catholic priests… and thereafter be brought up in the Catholic faith."

To understand what 'the galleys' were, take a look at the report of an eyewitness:

"It was strange to see so many hundreds of miserably naked persons, having their heads shaven, a pair of rough canvas drawers, their whole backs and legs naked, chained about by strokes of the whip on their backs and soles of their feet on the last disorder and without the least humanity."

Texts from J.A.P.Jones, The Early Modern World 1450-1700, MacMillan Education (London 1983) p. 190 f.

---

① Explain why the French king turned against the Huguenots.

_____

_____

_____

_____

M 2 "Secure and honest means ('moyens') to lead the heretics back to the Catholic belief."

② Describe the cartoon in detail. *See textbook, p. 91, "Analysing Cartoons".*

③ Match the six means of dealing with the Huguenots with the numbers in the cartoon. (1 – 2 – 3 – 4 – 5 – 6)

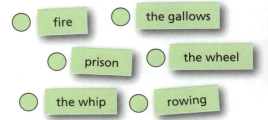

○ fire   ○ the gallows
○ prison   ○ the wheel
○ the whip   ○ rowing

| 1640 | 1655 | 1670 | 1685 | 1700 | 1715 | 1730 | 1745 | 1760 | 1775 | 1790 |

IV. Mercantilism

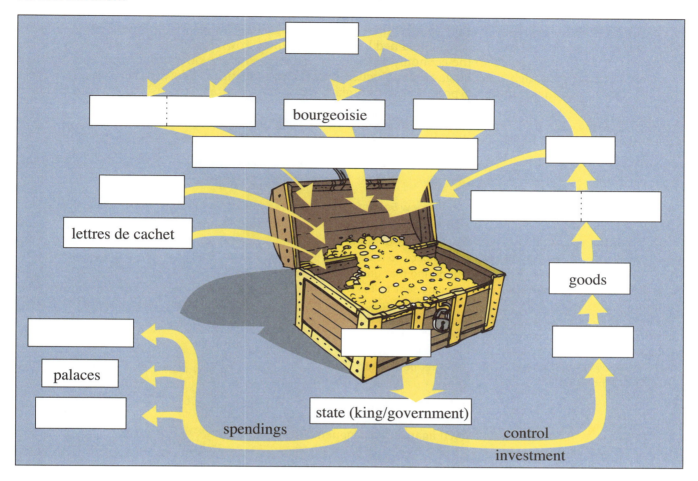

1. Fill in these terms:

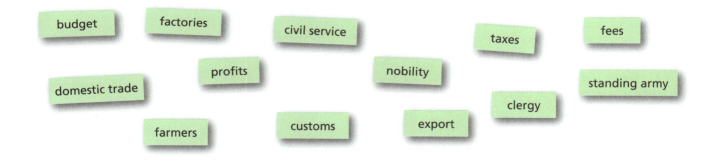

budget, factories, civil service, taxes, fees, profits, nobility, standing army, domestic trade, clergy, farmers, customs, export

2. Explain how Colbert's system of mercantilism worked *(see textbook, p. 12 f)*.

_____
_____
_____
_____

3. The system of mercantilism may go wrong in different ways. Mark where and explain why.

1. Absolutism and Enlightenment

V. The Image of the Monarch – Symbols of Power

- ◯ Sword of Charlemagne
- ◯ Column with relief
- ◯ Dancemaster – step appears artificial
- ◯ Left hand is put on the King's hip
- ◯ Necklace with the Order of the Golden Fleece
- ◯ Red shoes were only worn by the nobility
- ◯ Earnest and reserved official expression of the face
- ◯ Falling in folds of coat fit
- ◯ Lion-like wig makes person appear taller
- ◯ Canopy of red velvet frames the painting like a vault
- ◯ Sceptre in right hand is based on table with crown and 'main de justice'
- ◯ Table covered with blue velvet which shows the golden lily of the Bourbons

Louis XIV, painting by Hyacinthe Rigaud, about 1700

A Tradition   B Power   C Unity of person and office   D Dignity   E Elegance, cultivated lifestyle

① Put the numbers in the painting in the boxes in front of the definitions. There is a larger print of the painting in your textbook, p. 16.

② Colour the definitions 1–12 in the colour of the explanations A to E.

1640	1655	1670	1685	1700	1715	1730	1745	1760	1775	1790

VI. Louis's France – Revision

① Louis XIV was born in ▦ 1638 and died in ▦ 1661
  ▦ 1715 ▦ 1789
  ▦ 1661 ▦ 1715

② His most important advisors were (tick 3)
  ▦ Cardinal Richelieu ▦ Cardinal Bossuet ▦ Marshall Petain
  ▦ Minister Colbert ▦ Dr. Mercantile ▦ Cardinal Mazarin

③ According to Louis's most important advisor the only goal of the monarch had to be
  ▦ to earn a lot of money ▦ the public interest ▦ to fight against the enemies of France

④ Louis controlled many things directly. Name three of them:

_____

_____

⑤ Who belonged to which estate?

First Estate: _____ Second Estate: _____ Third Estate: _____

⑥ Louis's way of treating the Huguenots was written down in
  ▦ the Edict of Nantes ▦ the Edict of Paris ▦ the Edict of Fontainebleau

⑦ The Edict forced the Huguenots to _____

⑧ What did that mean for France?

_____

⑨ Louis's economic system was called _____

⑩ Its main aim was supposed to be ▦ buying and selling as much as possible
  ▦ achieving a positive balance of trade
  ▦ exporting raw material

⑪ The economic system was supported by various measures. Name six:

_____

_____

⑫ Louis's wars. Tick the most important reason for them and their most important result.
  reason: ▦ support of family members result: ▦ France was bankrupt
    ▦ policy of hegemony   ▦ France gained land
    ▦ defense of France   ▦ Louis became emperor

9

1. Absolutism and Enlightenment

VII. A Great Leap

M 1 The balloon of the Brothers Mongolfiere was a sensation for the people, who faced lots of new inventions in the 18th century.
Copper Etching 1783

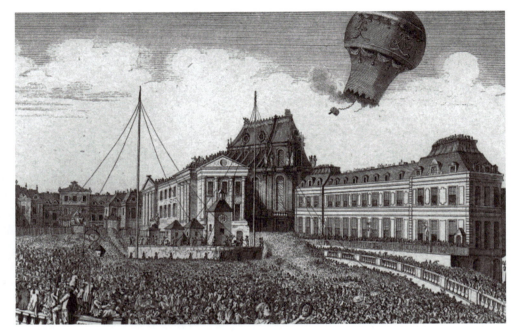

M 2 Inventions and Discoveries in the Age of Enlightenment:

1666	Newton's Gravitation Law
1693	Porcelain in Europe
1711	Three-Colour Printing
1718	Fahrenheit's Quicksilver Thermometer
1735	Cast Iron
1751–1777	Diderot's Encyclopaedia
1752	Lightning Conductor
1754	Sheet Metal Factories
1766	Hydrogen
1769	James Watt's Steam Engine
1771	Oxygen
1772	Nitrogen

1 Give a brief portrait of the Age of Enlightenment using the following terms:

natural sciences   energy   superstition   constitution   philosophy

_____
_____
_____
_____

2 Give your opinion about the reasons why people were so fascinated with the 'Mongolfiere'.

_____
_____
_____

| 1640 | 1655 | 1670 | 1685 | 1700 | 1715 | 1730 | 1745 | 1760 | 1775 | 1790 |

VIII. Frederick II, the Enlightened Monarch

M 1 **Frederick II and Farming**
The painting "King Everywhere" shows Frederick II checking if his orders about planting potatoes are followed.

M 2 **Frederick II, the Soldier**
Battle of Zorndorf, 1758

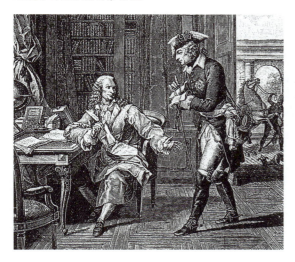

M 3 **Frederick II and Voltaire**
Frederick II and the French philosopher Voltaire having a discussion at Sanssouci.

① Find out the main message of each picture. See also "The Fluteplayer", textbook, p. 7.

② Explain why people's opinions of Frederick II are mixed.

③ Work out the difference between the roles Frederick II and Louis XIV played in their respective countries.

11

2. The American Revolution

I. National Treasures

① Match the following captions with the pictures:

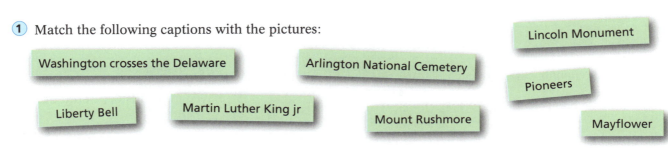

12

| 1580 | 1610 | 1640 | 1670 | 1700 | 1730 | 1760 | 1790 | 1820 | 1850 | 1880 |

2) Find out about the role the depicted items/incidents have played in the history of the USA.

3) Prepare a brief speech about each item.

13

2. The American Revolution

II. The Trail of Tears

M 1 "Trail of Tears" by Robert Lindneux, 1942

M 2

M 3 Georgia militiaman who participated in the 'round up' of the Cherokee Indians:
"I fought through the Civil War and have seen men shot to pieces and slaughtered by thousands, but the Cherokee removal was the cruellest work I ever knew."
http://www.cerritos.edu/soliver/American%20Identities/Trail%20of%20Tears/quotes.htm

M 4 Recollections of a survivor:
"Long time we travel on way to new land. People feel bad when they leave Old Nation. Womens cry and make sad wails. Children cry and many men cry…but they say nothing and just put heads down and keep on go towards West. Many days pass and people die very much."
http://www.nps.gov/trte/historyculture/stories.htm

① Describe the picture (*see textbook, p. 17, "Analysing Paintings"*).

_____

_____

_____

② Explain the information the map contains about the trail of the Cherokees.

_____

_____

③ 'Walk a mile' in one of the Cherokees' shoes. Write down his/her feelings and emotions like in a diary.

| 1580 | 1610 | 1640 | 1670 | 1700 | 1730 | 1760 | 1790 | 1820 | 1850 | 1880 |

III. The Course of American History – Revision

1 **The history of the USA can be divided into three phases. Match their names and dates by numbers 1–2–3.**
_____ pioneer phase   _____ from 1890 to today
_____ world power   _____ from 1607 to 1783
_____ colonial phase   _____ from 1783 to 1890

2 **The first settlers came to America because**   ▨ the weather was better than in England.
▨ they had been persecuted in England.
▨ they wanted to have slaves.

3 **The colonists**   ▨ had the same rights as English citizens.
▨ had the same rights as everybody else in the colonies.
▨ didn't have any rights and had to follow their priests' orders.

4 **The 'French and Indian War' from 1755 to 1763**   ▨ was won by the Indians.
▨ was won by France.
▨ was won by England.

5 **The Boston Massacre in** ▨ 1770 ▨ 1776 ▨ 1783 **was**
▨ an attack of the colonists on British soldiers, in which hundreds of soldiers were killed.
▨ an attack of the British soldiers on the colonists, in which five colonists were killed.
▨ an attack of Indians on the city of Boston, in which many colonists were killed.

6 **The Boston Tea Party in** ▨ 1770 ▨ 1773 ▨ 1776 **was**
▨ a demonstration of the colonists disguised as Native Americans against the Tea Act.
▨ an attempt of the Native Americans to get a few boxes of tea without paying.
▨ a demonstration of colonists and Native Americans against the Tea Act.

7 **At first the colonists only wanted**   ▨ representation without taxation.
▨ no representation and no taxation.
▨ no taxation without representation.

8 **The War of Independence broke out in** _____ **and ended in** _____ .

9 **The three most important rights the Americans got in the Declaration of Independence were**
▨ life   ▨ death   ▨ pursuit of happiness   ▨ liberty   ▨ free shopping   ▨ religion

10 **There were** ▨ 11 ▨ 12 ▨ 13 **original founder states**
which signed the constitution after ▨ 1776 ▨ 1783 ▨ 1789

11 **The former settlers conquered the area which is now called the USA because**
▨ they thought God had given them the right to do so.
▨ they wanted to hunt the buffalo.
▨ because they needed the land to survive.

12 **In the 19th century 'all men are created equal' applied to**   ▨ whites.
▨ whites and Native Americans.
▨ whites, blacks and Indians.

15

3. The French Revolution

I. The First Phase of the Revolution

1 Describe the situations in detail.

A

B

C

D

2 Analyse the artist's perspective and intention.

M 1 "Pictures of memorable incidents, which took place in France in the years 1789, 1790 and 1791".
Coloured woodcut distributed as a kind of picture paper.

3. The French Revolution

II. The King's Flight

1 Explain what the flight shows about the king's attitude to politics.

_____

_____

_____

_____

_____

_____

_____

2 Divide the reasons for the failing of the flight into

a) bad luck

_____

_____

_____

_____

b) mistakes by the runaways

_____

_____

_____

_____

3 Imagine you are a Parisian reporter and your editor asks you to comment briefly on the king's flight. Write your comment for the edition of the day after the flight.

_____

_____

_____

_____

_____

| 1770 | 1775 | 1780 | 1785 | 1790 | 1795 | 1800 | 1805 | 1810 | 1815 | 1820 |

M1 Comic from the English Textbook: Society in Changes, London 1992

4 Discuss whether it is a good idea to present a historical event in the form of a comic.

Pro

_____

_____

Con

_____

_____

3. The French Revolution

III. Was the Terror Necessary?

M 1 What the leaders of the Revolution said

a) From a newspaper article by Camille Desmoulins, a former school friend of Robespierre and a revolutionary journalist, December 1783:

"You want to remove all your enemies by means of the guillotine? […] Do you believe that these women, these old men, these weaklings […] are really dangerous?"

b) Written by Marat. He was partly responsible for the September massacres in 1792:

"No one hates the spilling of blood more than I do, but to prevent floods of it from flowing, I urge you to pour out a few drops. Eleven months ago 500 heads would have been enough. Today 50000 would be necessary. Perhaps 80000 will fall before the end of the year. France will be flooded with blood."

M 2 What outsiders said

From a speech by Charles J. Fox, a British politician, November 1793. He had been a great supporter of the Revolution until the September massacres:

"What a pity that the French, who are capable of such great energy, should be governed by those who are guilty of such unheard of crimes and cruelties."

M 3 What French people said

Extracts from police reports in Paris, early 1794:

"a) The majority of the citizens agreed unanimously that the tribunals act well, that they let the innocent go and punish the guilty.
b) Bitter complaints were repeated today of the arrest and imprisonment of citizens who are good patriots and who are victims of ambition, greed and jealousy.
c) On seeing peasants on the scaffold, people said, 'Why have these wretches allowed themselves to be corrupted? If they were nobles or rich people it would not be strange their being counter-revolutionaries, but in that class we should expect all to be supporters of the Revolution.'"

M 4 What modern historians have said

a) Written by R. R. Palmer, a modern historian. He is describing the France of 1793 and trying to explain why the Terror happened at all, 1989:

"Anarchy within. Invasion without…War. Inflation. Hunger. Fear. Hate. Sabotage. Fantastic hopes… And the horrible knowledge for the men in power that if they failed they would die as criminals and murderers of their king, and all the gains of the Revolution would be lost, and the faith that if they won they would bring liberty, equality and fraternity into their world."

b) Written by Robert Darnton, an American, 1989:

"By twentieth-century standards the Terror was not very big. It took about 17000 lives. There were fewer than 25 executions in half the departments of France, none at all in six of them."

M 5 Victims of the Terror, 1793

① Work out the main message of each text and the painting.

② Whose side are you on? Explain your reasons and your view of things.

IV. The 16 Steps of the Revolution

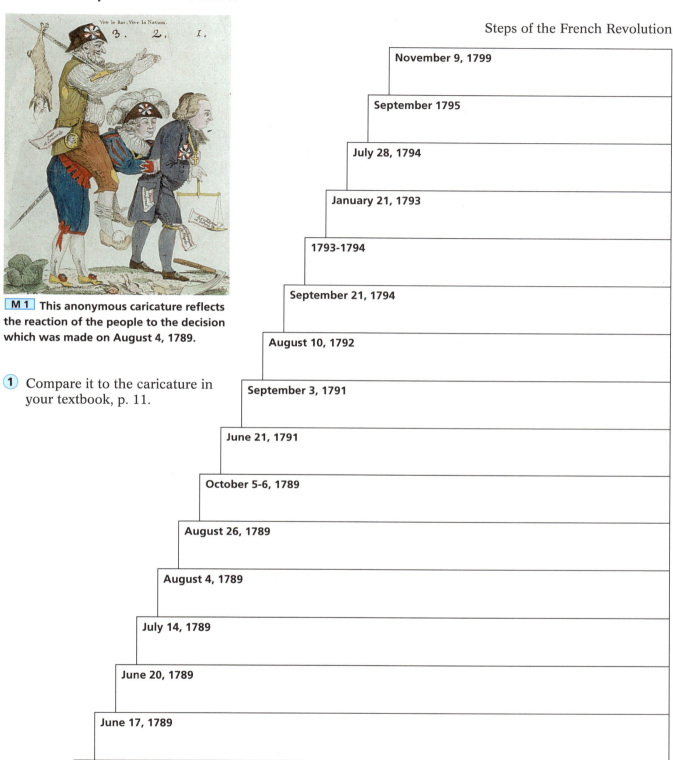

M 1 This anonymous caricature reflects the reaction of the people to the decision which was made on August 4, 1789.

① Compare it to the caricature in your textbook, p. 11.

Steps of the French Revolution

- November 9, 1799
- September 1795
- July 28, 1794
- January 21, 1793
- 1793-1794
- September 21, 1794
- August 10, 1792
- September 3, 1791
- June 21, 1791
- October 5-6, 1789
- August 26, 1789
- August 4, 1789
- July 14, 1789
- June 20, 1789
- June 17, 1789
- May 5, 1789

② Several important incidents mark the course of the French Revolution. They are shown as single steps indicating their dates. Fill in the events using note form and point out briefly what their consequences were. You will find the dates in your textbook.

21

3. The French Revolution

V. Napoleon's Rise and Downfall

M 1 Picture from 1814

Pictures like these were traditionally made to show a person's rise and fall, but also to symbolize transience, the idea that nothing will remain forever.
These were the labels used by the artist to characterize Napoleon's stages in life:

| General | Emperor | Purgatory | Corsican boy | Return from Spain |

| Sleighride from Moscow | Ruler | Gambler in Paris | Farewell from Germany |

| Termination | Army Training |

① Match them with Napoleon's life.

② Analyse what the caricature shows about the artist's attitude towards Napoleon.

_____
_____
_____

③ Find out about the nationality of the artist. Prove your opinion.

_____
_____
_____

VI. Reforms in Prussia

1 Here are the portraits of four important Prussian reformers, two of which can be found in your textbook. The other two are Gerhard of Scharnhorst and William of Humboldt, who were responsible for the reforms of education and of the military. Find out who is who and who did what. Then investigate into the other dates and facts and fill them in.

*   †   *   †   *   †   *   †

2 Tick the right answer:

A By the 1807 edict on the liberation of the farmers
- the Prussian nobility lost all their land.
- the hereditary dependence of the farmers were abolished.
- the farmers did not have to pay back their debts.
- the Prussian nobility was abolished.

B By the introduction of the new constitutions of the towns
- the mayors, who were appointed by the king, got more rights.
- public order and the rights of the police were changed.
- all people in Prussia were allowed to freely choose their profession and their job.
- the self-government of the towns by elected town councillors was introduced.

C By the reform of the military
- the tried and tested army was made bigger and got new weapons.
- a people's army was formed because of universal military service.
- the well-known corporal punishment was improved.
- the soldiers received the same weapons and the uniforms of the French troops.

D By the reform of education
- women got access to the schools and universities of the country.
- the talents and abilities of the people were to be improved for the good of the state.
- compulsory school attendance was first introduced.
- school fees were abolished.

E The Prussian reforms were the precondition for
- Prussia's joining the Confederation of the Rhine.
- King Frederick William III's crown.
- the continuing differences between the estates.
- the growth of the Prussian economy and her military strength.

4. Industrialization

I. Population Explosion

By 1800 Malthus's ideas did not apply any longer, because the number of people outgrew what he called the "natural limit" or "population ceiling". Look at the different aspects.

Agriculture
Because of farming changes in the 18th cent., farmers could produce more milk, cheese and vegetables.

Environment
At the beginning of the 18th cent., many marshes were dried up; this killed many mosquitoes, so fewer people got malaria.

Culture
At the beginning of the 18th cent., drinking gin was very popular. This changed after the government put tax on gin in 1751. Gin can cause women to lose their unborn babies and can damage unborn babies.

Government
The Public Health Acts in 1848 and 1875 improved housing and public health in urban areas.

Climate
After 1780, it became warmer, which was helpful in farming.

Factories
After 1780, more children worked in factories. This was good for the families, because they earned money.

Hygiene
After 1790, soap became cheaper and it was easier to get.

Fashion
After 1750, people began to wear cotton, in stead of wool. Cotton is easier to wash.

Society
After 1700, people married earlier, and fewer people stayed unmarried.

Birth
In the 18th cent., pregnant women were better cared for and there were other improvements so it was safer for women to give birth.

Medicine
In 1796, vaccination was discovered and people were vaccinated against smallpox.

1 List the aspects you think could reduce mortality (the number of deaths)?

_____

_____

_____

2 List the aspects you think could increase the birthrate (the number of births)?

_____

_____

_____

3 Be prepared to explain your findings in class.

24

| 1765 | 1780 | 1805 | 1820 | 1835 | 1850 | 1865 | 1880 | 1895 | 1910 | 1925 |

II. Revolution in Transport

Travelling in 1850			
Distance in km		Duration of journey in hours	
from Berlin	to	by coach	by train
300	Hamburg	<50	~7,5
290	Hannover	<42	~6
150	Stettin	<17	~3
160	Leipzig	<19	~5,5
350	Breslau	<40	~6
440	Nuremberg	<40	~10
570	Cologne	<85	~11
160	Dresden	<25	~3,5

M 1

1 Show by what percentage travelling times to the above eight places were reduced.

Hamburg	Hannover	Stettin	Leipzig

Breslau	Nuremberg	Cologne	Dresden

2 List reasons why this new means of transportation was so attractive.

_____

_____

_____

_____

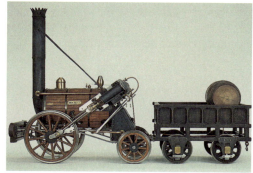

3 Assess the consequences of the new travelling times for the people.

_____

_____

_____

_____

4 Find out when the railways were built in or near your town.

_____

_____

_____

M 2 The invention of the steam engine by George Stephenson in 1814 ("The Rocket", top picture) started a new chapter in the history of transport. In the bottom picture there is "Beuth", a steam engine build by Borsig, a German industrialist, in 1843.

25

4. Industrialization

III. Triumph of Electricity

M 1 This postcard was printed in 1891 for an electricity exhibition in Frankfurt.

1. List what the five people in the postcard symbolize.

2. What is the message of this postcard?

3. List inventions that were only possible because of electricity.

4. Which industrial branches were especially improved by electricity?

| 1765 | 1780 | 1805 | 1820 | 1835 | 1850 | 1865 | 1880 | 1895 | 1910 | 1925 |

IV. Living Conditions – Housing

M1 **A family in their apartment in a working class district of Berlin,** 1907

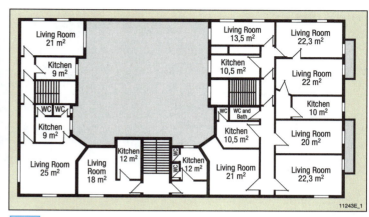

M2 **Floorplan of a tenement house, Berlin,** about 1905

(1) Compare the photo of the working class family with a photo of your own famliy.

_____

_____

_____

_____

_____

_____

(2) Draw the floorplan of your house/apartment and compare it to the one shown above (M2).

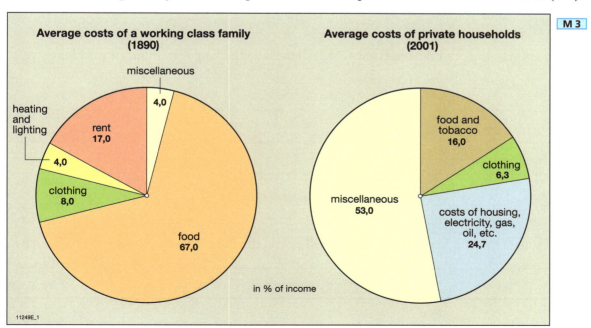

M3

(3) As you have learned to analyse statistics *(see textbook, p. 70 f, "Analysing Statistics")*, use the guiding tasks and questions on p. 71 to interpret and present the graphs above.

27

4. Industrialization

V. Child Labour

M1

M2 Many people who visited the factories were horrified. In 1831-32 a Commission of Parliament was set up and hundreds of people who worked in the mills were interviewed. Here are some extracts of these interviews:

Charles Burn, aged 14; he began work at the age of eight:
How often were you allowed to go to the toilet? – Three times a day.
Were you allowed to go to the toilet at any time you wanted? – No; only when a boy came to tell you it was your turn.

James Carpenter, Leeds millhand:
What means were taken to keep the children to their work? – Sometimes they would tap them over the head, or nip them over the nose, or throw water in their faces, or shake them about to keep them awake.

Mark Best, an overlooker:
Were the children fined as well as beaten sometimes? – Yes. For various things; if they were caught combing their hair before they went home, or washing themselves … they would not even allow them to speak to one another.

Joseph Badder, an overlooker:
I have often had complaints against myself by the parents of children for beating them. […] I'm sure that no man can do without it who works long hours. I told them I was very sorry after I had done it, but I was forced to do it. The master expected me to do my work, and I could not do mine unless they did theirs.

Joseph Hebergam; he had worked since he was seven:
When I had worked about half a year, a weakness fell into my knees and ankles. In the morning I could scarcely walk, and my brother and sister used out of kindness to take me under each arm and run with me, a good mile, to the mill, and my legs dragged on the ground because of the pain; I could not walk. If we were five minutes too late, the overlooker would take a strap, and beat us till we were black and blue.

from John D. Clare: The Age of Expansion 1750-1914. Nelson, Surrey et al. 1996, p. 55

① Look at the pictures (M1) and read the interviews (M2). Describe the living conditions of working children.

_____
_____
_____
_____

② Imagine you were one of the children in the pictures. Tell one of the interviewers what your average day looks like.

_____
_____
_____

| 1765 | 1780 | 1805 | 1820 | 1835 | 1850 | 1865 | 1880 | 1895 | 1910 | 1925 |

3 Please fill in the missing words from this list:

The text is taken from a FACTORY ACT passed in Parliament in 1833:

Children under 9 must not be _____ .

Children aged 9 – 13 may only work nine hours _____ .

Children aged 13 – 16 may only work _____ a day.

No one under 18 years is to work _____ .

Every child must have two hours' _____ a day.

Four government inspectors will _____ the factories.

> employed
>
> inspect
>
> a day
>
> teaching
>
> 12 hours
>
> at night

4 Comment on the following statement of a factory owner:
"After all, there are no birth certificates. Who can tell how old these children really are?"

_____

_____

_____

_____

5 Read the UNICEF report and the definitions of "child labour" and "child work". Show whether the situation for children has changed. Give reasons for your answer.

_____

_____

_____

_____

_____

_____

M 3 **Child Work versus Child Labour**

Child work: Children's participation in economic activity – that does not negatively affect their health and development or interfere with education, can be positive. Work that does not interfere with education (light work) is permitted from the age of 12 years under the International Labour Organization (ILO) Convention 138.

Child labour: This is more narrowly defined and refers to children working in contravention of the above standards. This means all children below 12 years of age working in any economic activities, those aged 12 to 14 years engaged in harmful work, and all children engaged in the worst forms of child labour.

Worst forms of child labour: These involve children being enslaved, forcibly recruited, prostituted, trafficked, forced into illegal activities and exposed to hazardous work.

http://www.unicef.org/protection/index_childlabour.html

6 Find out what the situation of child labour is today.

_____

_____

7 Daniel Radcliffe was 11 years old when he played Harry Potter in the first of the Harry Potter films. Since then he has often worked for many hours, at times for several days a week. The amount of money he earns is considerable. Daniel Radcliffe himself says he enjoys acting and does not consider it "work". Discuss.

4. Industrialization

VI. The Strike

M 1 **The Strike,** by Robert Köhler, 1886

1 Describe the atmosphere of the painting.

| 1765 | 1780 | 1805 | 1820 | 1835 | 1850 | 1865 | 1880 | 1895 | 1910 | 1925 |

② The following table will help you to describe the painting "The Strike" by R. Köhler in great detail *(see textbook, p. 16f, "Analysing Paintings")*. For each of the numbered persons write down what they are doing (action), where they are in the picture (location), what they are wearing (outfit), and how and in what way they are related to other people in the painting (relation to others).

people	action	location	outfit	relation to others
1				
2				
3				
4				
5				
6				
7				
8				
9				

③ Sum up all your findings and discuss the artist's message.

_____

_____

_____

_____

_____

_____

_____

4. Industrialization

VII. Social Security

In 1883 Bismarck initiated health insurance for workers, followed by accident insurance in 1884 and old age and invalidity insurance in 1889 to relieve the misery of the working people. The poster from 1913 shows how these insurances developed over time.

1. Explain the social security system of 1913 in each section.

___

2. Give reasons for the headline "The German Social Security System is the world's leading role model".

___

3. Find out about our social security system today and discuss our problems with it.

| 1765 | 1780 | 1805 | 1820 | 1835 | 1850 | 1865 | 1880 | 1895 | 1910 | 1925 |

VIII. Summary – From Cottage Industry to Factory Industry

1 Read the text below carefully. Use the following words to fill in the blanks.

> undertaken, sheep-farming, 18th century, profits, regular wages, demand, by hand, be woven, various machines, set routines, joined in, woollen, cottage industry, factory industry, branch

At the beginning of the _____ most people living in Britain were farmers. Many of them did other work as well. Goods were made _____. People worked in their own houses in villages, often the whole family was involved: Father, mother and children; all _____. Even three-year-old youngsters were expected to earn money. This system is known as _____. The biggest _____ of all was the making of _____ cloth. Making cloth from wool involves two processes: 1 The wool must be spun into a thread. 2 The thread must _____ into cloth.

As there were many _____ areas, there was plenty of wool that could be turned into cloth. This was _____ in the workers' homes. People worked long hours at this in dark, cramped rooms. However, despite the hard work they had to do, they could decide what hours they worked. As the population grew, so did the _____ for cloth. British merchants wanted to increase their _____ by making more cloth in Britain. But the cottage industry was slow and inefficient. Throughout the 18th century _____ were invented to make the above-mentioned processes faster. The new machines could not be used in ordinary cottages. So the cloth-making industry was the first to change from a cottage industry to a _____. From now onwards people worked in large factories in towns and followed _____ of work. Between 1750 – 1850 more and more people moved to towns to get work in these new facotries. They were pleased to get work and to get _____. However, the conditions of work there were often terrible.

2 a) Solve the crossword puzzle below. The letters in the red boxes will help you to complete the solution.
b) Assess the question that is the solution to the crossword puzzle.
c) Discuss your conclusion with your class.

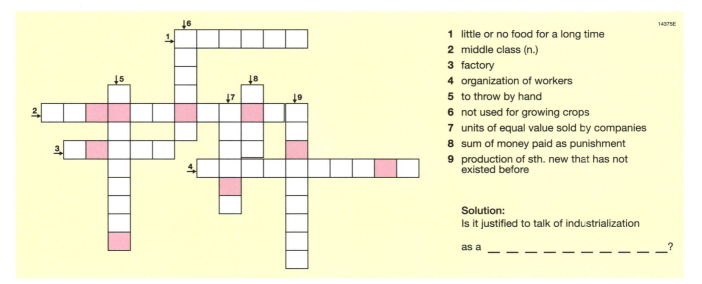

1 little or no food for a long time
2 middle class (n.)
3 factory
4 organization of workers
5 to throw by hand
6 not used for growing crops
7 units of equal value sold by companies
8 sum of money paid as punishment
9 production of sth. new that has not existed before

Solution:
Is it justified to talk of industrialization as a _ _ _ _ _ _ _ _ _ _ ?

5. The Struggle for Unity and Liberty

I. The Congress of Vienna and the Holy Alliance

1 Match the principles of the Congress of Vienna with their meanings.

_____ restoration	A. the rulers in Europe would prevent any power from becoming more powerful than the others
_____ legitimacy	B. the rulers were to work together to keep unrest in check
_____ compensation	C. the powers would return to the political situation as it existed before 1792
_____ the balance of power	D. the rulers who had been in charge before 1792 were to be returned to power
_____ solidarity among the sovereigns	E. lost territory was to be returned, or at least paid for in some way (usually by annexing new territory)

2 Explain the disappointment of nationals and liberals with the Congress.

_____

_____

_____

On 26 September 1815 the "Holy Alliance" among the monarchs of Russia, Prussia and Austria was signed. Its purpose was to maintain dynastic traditions, the principle of legitimacy and the unity of the throne and the altar. The monarchs also agreed to help each other deal with revolutionary situations within or outside of their countries.

3 Describe the painting briefly *(see textbook, p. 17, "Analysing Paintings")*, using the following terms.

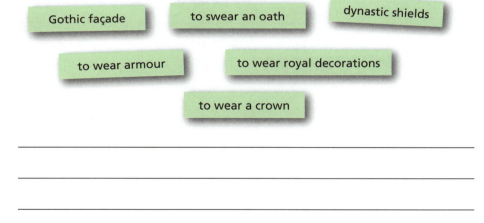

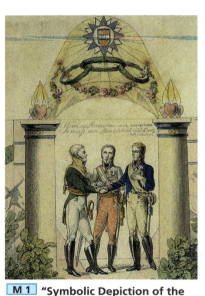

M 1 "Symbolic Depiction of the Holy Alliance", painting by Heinrich Olivier, 1815
The three monarchs Frederick William III of Prussia, Francis I of Austria and Tsar Alexander I of Russia unite.

_____

_____

_____

_____

4 Name principles of the Congress of Vienna which the alliance partners promised to uphold and point out aspects which refer to these principles in the painting.

_____

_____

34

| 1810 | 1815 | 1820 | 1825 | 1830 | 1835 | 1840 | 1845 | 1850 | 1855 | 1860 |

II. Political Murder

M 1 The Assassination of August von Kotzebue, 23 March 1819

① List details of the murder which you can see in the picture.

_____
_____
_____

② At the time, some nationalists claimed that Sand (who was executed for his crime) had died for German liberty. Others weren't so certain. How controversial would a crime like Sand's be today? Explain your thinking.

_____
_____
_____
_____

③ Comment on forms of political resistance which you find acceptable.

_____
_____
_____

④ Look at the examples of unrest in Germany and determine which events were violent and which were non-violent.

event	violent	non-violent
founding the student societies, 1818		
the Wartburg Festival, 1817		
the murder of Kotzebue, 1819		
the Hambach Festival, 1832		
the complaint of the Göttingen Seven		

35

5. The Struggle for Unity and Liberty

III. The Frankfurt Parliament, 1848-49

Different Social Origins

\	Members of the Frankfurt Parliament in 1848
number	occupation
1) academic and self-employed professionals	
94	professors at universities and upper-level schools
30	teachers
39	pastors
106	lawyers
23	medical doctors
3	librarians
7	publishers, booksellers
20	writers
35	other university graduates
2) state and local civil servants	
18	military officers
11	diplomats
110	judges, state's attorneys
115	higher administrative officials
21	mayors
37	mid-level civil servants
3) businessmen	
46	farmers
35	merchants
14	factory owners
4	artisans
4) others	
44	occupation unknown
812	total

\	Killed in the Berlin March Uprising, 1848
number	occupation
14	workers (12 men, 2 women)
6	domestic servants
1	maker of leather goods
1	innkeeper
1	merchant
1	administrative intern
1	border policeman
1	railway inspector
1	higher tax inspector's daughter
59	artisans, journeymen and apprentices
35	different artisans, including 5 fabric printers, 4 tailors, 4 mechanics, 3 mechanical engineers, 3 shoemakers, 2 smiths, 2 paperhangers
0	occupation unknown
121	**total (in this list)**

1 Fill in the following tables with the absolute numbers and percentages of the social origins of the members of the Frankfurt Parliament and of the Berlin uprising's dead. Use these categories:

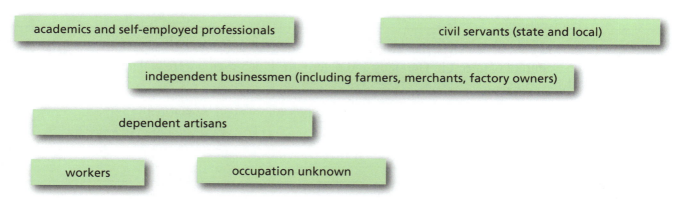

academics and self-employed professionals

civil servants (state and local)

independent businessmen (including farmers, merchants, factory owners)

dependent artisans

workers

occupation unknown

Members of the Frankfurt Parliament in 1848		
social origins	absolute numbers	per cent
academics and professionals		
civil servants		
independent businessmen		
dependent artisans		
workers		
occupation unknown		
total		

Killed in the Berlin March Uprising, 1848		
social origins	absolute numbers	per cent
academics and professionals		
civil servants		
independent businessmen		
dependent artisans		
workers		
occupation unknown		
total		

Enter the two bar charts here:

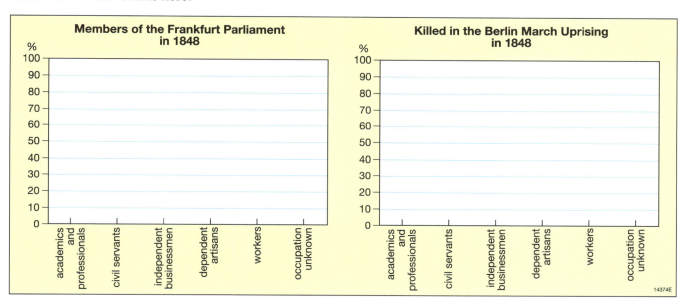

2 Comment on the differences in the social origins of the two groups.

_____

_____

_____

3 Point out how the differences in the groups affected the Frankfurt Parliament in 1848-49.

_____

_____

_____

5. The Struggle for Unity and Liberty

IV. Debates in the Assembly

M 1 Deputy Piepmeyer gives a speech
Caricature by Johann Hermann Detmold and Adolf Schrödter, 1848

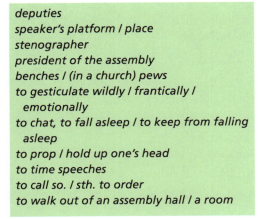

deputies
speaker's platform / place
stenographer
president of the assembly
benches / (in a church) pews
to gesticulate wildly / frantically / emotionally
to chat, to fall asleep / to keep from falling asleep
to prop / hold up one's head
to time speeches
to call so. / sth. to order
to walk out of an assembly hall / a room

M 2 Deputy Baumstark steps up to the podium
(from "Kladderadatsch", November 1848)

steps to speaker's platform
hats, walking sticks on the benches
to flee from sth.
coattails flying
to jump / leap over benches

See textbook, p. 91, "Analysing Cartoons", to help you with these tasks.

1 Describe both cartoons briefly.

	M1	M2
objects / people:		
caption / title:		
main words / phrases:		
dates:		
other aspects:		

1810	1815	1820	1825	1830	1835	1840	1845	1850	1855	1860

2 Assess the information about the Frankfurt Parliament given in both cartoons.

	M1	M2
symbols used:		
meaning of symbols:		
words used and why important:		
adjectives to describe emotions:		

3 Interpret the cartoons.

	M1	M2
Describe the actions taking place.		
Show how the words clarify the situation.		
Explain the message.		
Identify those who agree or disagree with the cartoon's message.		

4 Agree or disagree with the cartoonists' criticism of the Frankfurt Parliament in 1848, explaining your reasons.

_____

_____

_____

5 Comment on the opinion of the Frankfurt Parliament which cartoons like these made popular in 1848.

_____

_____

_____

6. Imperial Germany

I. Proclamation of the German Empire, 1871

A Famous Painting: Fact or Fiction?

Anton von Werner was commissioned to paint a picture, "The Proclamation of the German Emperor at the Palace of Versailles in 1871", and he was present at the event. During the short ceremony he could only make a few sketches. His painting was made as a present for Bismarck on his seventieth birthday in 1885. It hangs on display today in the Bismarck Museum in Friedrichsruhe near Hamburg.

An earlier painting, made in 1877, was given to Emperor William I as a present on his eightieth birthday. It is known today as the "palace version". This painting was destroyed in World War II. Today we have only a black and white photograph of it. A comparison of the photograph with the Friedrichsruhe painting reveals many interesting details.

podium
men in uniforms
to wear sashes
 (to show their
 high rank)
flags of the German
 states
mirrors on the walls
to wave swords /
 to raise their arms /
 to cheer s.o. or
 s.th.
in the foreground
 /background

M 1 The "Palace" Painting, 1877

Note:
The princes stand on the podium, officers stand on the floor.
Bismarck is in white.
Baden raises his right arm.
The crown prince looks into the crowd.
Minister of War von Roon is shown, although he was absent.
General von Moltke holds up his hat in salute.
Others raise their swords.

M 2 The "Friedrichsruhe" Painting, 1885.

1855	1860	1865	1870	1875	1880	1885	1890	1895	1900	1905

Now compare both paintings (see textbook, p. 17, "Analysing Paintings").

1 Describe the painting.

	M1 palace painting	**M2** Friedrichsruhe painting
artist		
date of the picture		
size of the painting	no longer exists	167 x 202 cm
event shown and when		
number of people shown		
their actions and body language		
person who ordered it		
person who paid for it		
the perspective		

2 Analyse the painting.

	M1 palace painting	**M2** Friedrichsruhe painting
Find the main persons and their positions in the painting.		
Explain the elements of the persons' dress.		
Look for symbols and explain their significance.		
Note the observer's perspective.		

3 Interpret the painting.

	M1 palace painting	**M2** Friedrichsruhe painting
Assess the historical accuracy of the painting.		
State the artist's message in this painting.		

6. Imperial Germany

II. Differences in Voting in Germany and Prussia

Differences in Voting Laws and Their Consequences in Germany after 1871

Reichstag elections were based on the German Constitution of 1849. This voting system was used in elections to the North German parliament and later for the Reichstag. The 1869 electoral law for the North German Confederation applied to national elections and did not change from 1871 to 1918. Voting was universal, equal and direct – at the time it was the most advanced voting system in all of Europe. Usually, German men over the age of twenty-five living in one of the federal states could vote. Deputies were elected directly if they won the absolute majority of votes in their districts. (A second round was held if a majority was not reached in the first round.) Ballots were cast in secret and each vote counted equally. Apart from adding fifteen districts for Alsace-Lorraine in 1873, voting districts (set up with about 100,000 inhabitants in 1864) were not reapportioned until 1918. So the districts did not adapt to the extreme changes of the Industrial Revolution (farm workers moved into cities, workers moved from the east to the west of the country, and urbanization grew). By 1912, the electoral district Teltow near Berlin with 338,900 voters elected one deputy, while the district of Schaumburg-Lippe with only 10,700 voters also elected a deputy.

1 Fill in the column for the per cent of deputies elected to seats:

party	Reichstag election 1907		
	% of votes	deputies (number)	% of seats
Social Democrats	28.9 %	43	
Liberals	25.4 %	103	
Centre Party	19.4 %	105	
Conservatives	13.6 %	84	
others	12.6 %	62	
total	99.9 %	397	100.0 %

2 Now fill in the bar graph for 1907:

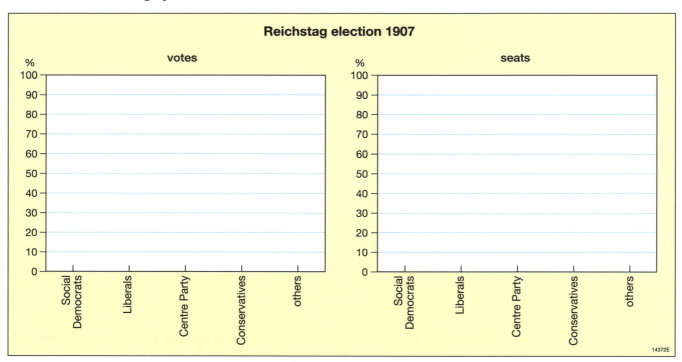

| 1855 | 1860 | 1865 | 1870 | 1875 | 1880 | 1885 | 1890 | 1895 | 1900 | 1905 |

The Prussian Three-Class Voting System
The other federal states had voting laws which were quite different. Most had a system based on classes. Prussia, for example, had a three-class electoral system which was used in Prussian (not German) elections. The idea was to give those taxpayers who paid higher taxes more of a voice in political affairs than those who paid less. The system divided the voters in each district into three classes – each class paid one-third of the direct taxes assessed in the voting district. The voting was indirect, oral (until 1906) and unequal. Each class voted for electors, who in turn voted for the actual deputies. This led to grotesque election results. In 1908, for example, the first class had only 3.8 % of all voters, the second class had 13.9 % of all voters, and the third class had 82.3 %. The districts were reapportioned in 1860 for the last time.

3 Fill in the column for the per cent of seats elected:

| Election to Prussian House of Deputies 1908 ||||
party	% of votes	no. of seats	% of seats
Social Democrats	23.9 %	6	
Liberals	17.5 %	102	
Centre Party	19.9 %	103	
Conservatives	17.2 %	215	
others	14.2 %	17	
unknown	7.2 %	0	
total	99.9 %	443	100.0 %

4 Fill in the bar graph:

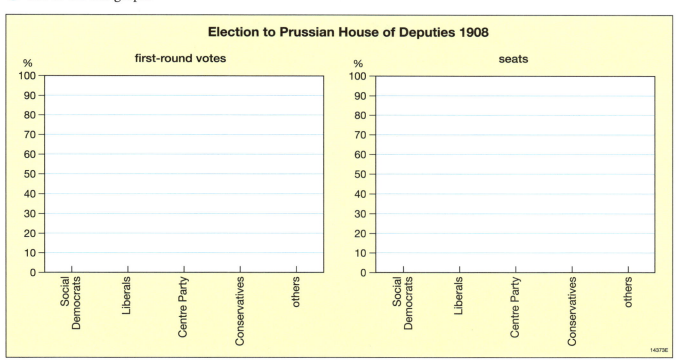

5 Now sum up the differences between the voting system for the Reichstag and the Prussian three-class voting system, referring to the elections of 1907 and 1908, in your notebook.

6. Imperial Germany

III. The Socialist Law and the End of the Kulturkampf

A British view of the Kulturkampf and Socialist Law in Germany

M 1 This cartoon from "Punch", published on 25 January 1879, is titled "'Of One Mind.'(For Once!)".

> to lean against a door
> to put a foot in a door
> to carry a torch
> to be of one mind
> to wear a white cap
> a cassock (traditionally worn by priests or monks)
> jackboots

1855	1860	1865	1870	1875	1880	1885	1890	1895	1900	1905

See textbook, p. 91, "Analysing Cartoons", for guidelines to help you do the following tasks.

1 Describe the cartoon briefly.

_____

_____

_____

_____

_____

_____

2 Assess the information given about the situation in Germany.

_____

_____

_____

_____

_____

_____

3 Interpret the cartoon.

_____

_____

_____

_____

_____

_____

_____

_____

_____

_____

_____

6. Imperial Germany

IV. Women's Suffrage

Women's Suffrage – John Stuart Mill versus Sigmund Freud
The question of women's rights raised in Germany was discussed throughout Europe at the same time. John Stuart Mill, a prominent British proponent of women's rights, was elected to Parliament in 1865 and was the first MP to call for women's voting rights. His book on the subject, "The Subjection of Women", was translated into German by Sigmund Freud, later known for his work in psychoanalysis. The two men had different views on the subject of women's rights.

M 1 John Stuart Mill, "The Subjection of Women", 1869

"But, it will be said, the rule of men over women [is not] a rule of force: it is accepted voluntarily; women make no complaint, and are consenting parties to it. In the first place, a great number of women do not accept it. Ever since there have been women able to make their sentiments known by their writings (the only mode of publicity which society permits to them), an increasing number of them have recorded protests against their present social condition: and recently many thousands of them, headed by the most eminent women known to the public, have petitioned Parliament for their admission to the *Parliamentary Suffrage*. [...] Nor is it only in our own country and in America that women are beginning to protest, more or less collectively, against the disabilities under which they labour. France, and Italy, and Switzerland, and Russia now afford examples of the same thing. How many more women there are who silently *cherish* similar aspirations, no one can possibly know; but there are *abundant tokens* how many **would** cherish them, were they not so strenuously taught to repress them as contrary to *the proprieties* of their sex."

http://oll.libertyfund.org/?option=com_staticxt&staticfile=show.php%3Ftitl e=347&chapter=5983&layout=html&Itemid=27

Parliamentary Suffrage: the right to vote for members of Parliament
to cherish: to love, appreciate
abundant: many
token: sign, symbol
the proprieties: accepted standards of politeness

M 2 Sigmund Freud, excerpt from a letter to his fiancée, 1883

"[Mill...] lacked in many matters the sense of the absurd; for example, in that of female emancipation and in the woman's question altogether.
I recollect that in the essay I translated a prominent argument was that a married woman could earn as much as her husband. We surely agree that the management of a house, the care and bringing up of children, demand the whole of a human being and almost excludes any earning, even if a simplified household relieve her of dusting, cleaning, cooking, etc. He had simply forgotten all that, like everything else concerning the relationship between the sexes.
[...] In his whole presentation it never emerges that women are different beings - we will not say lesser, rather the opposite - from men. He finds the suppression of women an analogy to that of Negroes. Any girl [...] whose hand a man kisses and for whose love he is prepared to dare all, could have set him right [...]
I believe that all reforming action in law and education would break down in front of the fact that, long before the age at which a man can earn a position in society, Nature has determined woman's destiny through beauty, charm, and sweetness. Law and custom have much to give women that has been withheld from them, but the position of women will surely be what it is: in youth an adored darling and in mature years a loved wife."

http://www.mdx.ac.uk/WWW/STUDY/xfremil.htm [26 October 2007]. Translated by Ernest Jones in "The Life and Work of Sigmund Freud", Penguin edition p. 166f.

| 1855 | 1860 | 1865 | 1870 | 1875 | 1880 | 1885 | 1890 | 1895 | 1900 | 1905 |

See textbook, p. 47, "Analysing Sources", for guidelines to help you do the following tasks.

1 Describe both texts.

_____

_____

_____

_____

_____

2 Analyse the texts.

_____

_____

_____

_____

_____

3 Evaluate the texts.

_____

_____

_____

_____

_____

_____

_____

_____

_____

_____

_____

_____

_____

7. New Imperialism and the Scramble for Africa

I. Personality: Emperor William II of Germany (1859-1941)

M1 **William II at the launch of the battleship „Wittelsbach", 1900:**

"The ocean is indispensable for Germany's greatness. But the ocean also proves that even far away and beyond it no great decision may be taken without Germany and the German Emperor."

http://www.preussen-chronik.de/_/ereignis_jsp/key=chronologie_008570.html

canopy
jackboots
sash or scarf
medals

M2 **Painting by Ludwig Noster,** Oil on canvas, 1900, 230,5 x 136,5 cm, Stadtmuseum Köln

| 1870 | 1875 | 1880 | 1885 | 1890 | 1895 | 1900 | 1905 | 1910 | 1915 | 1920 |

1 Describe the painting *(see textbook, p.17, "Analysing Paintings")*. Use the following terms: in the background/foreground, at the bottom/top, in the centre, on the left/right).

2 Discuss what message William II wanted to convey with this painting.

3 How does the message match the quote by William II in 1900?

4 Do some research on William´s life (Internet, encyclopedia) and list the main stages. Do you think he lived a happy life?

49

7. New Imperialism and the Scramble for Africa

II. The "New Course"

M 1 "The South Seas are the Mediterranean of the Future," Kladderadatsch (July 13, 1884)

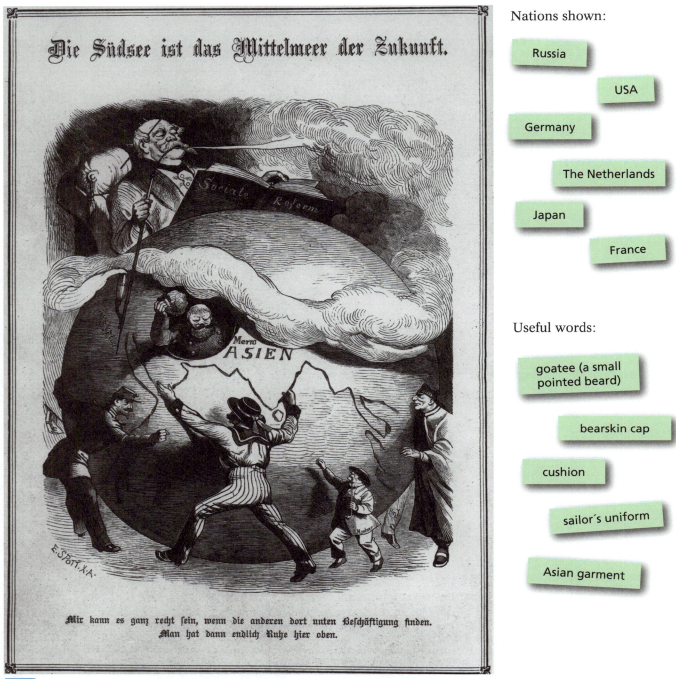

M 2 "That's fine with me, if the other powers are busy down there. Finally, it's quiet up here."

Nations shown:
- Russia
- USA
- Germany
- The Netherlands
- Japan
- France

Useful words:
- goatee (a small pointed beard)
- bearskin cap
- cushion
- sailor's uniform
- Asian garment

50

1870	1875	1880	1885	1890	1895	1900	1905	1910	1915	1920

M3 **A speech by Emperor William II to the North German Regatta Association, 1901.**

"… we have conquered for ourselves a place in the sun. It will now be my task to see to it that this place in the sun shall remain our undisputed possession, in order that the sun's rays may fall fruitfully upon our activity and trade in foreign parts… The more Germans go out upon the waters, …whether it be in journeys across the ocean, or in the service of the battle flag, so much the better it will be for us."

(http://www.fordham.edu/halsall/mod/1901kaiser.html)

1 Describe the cartoon *(see textbook, p.91, "Analysing Cartoons")*.

_____

_____

_____

_____

_____

_____

_____

_____

_____

2 Explain the message of the cartoon.

_____

_____

_____

_____

_____

3 Read the quote above and compare Emperor William's ideas to Bismarck's concept of imperialism as presented in the cartoon.

_____

_____

_____

_____

_____

_____

III. German Colonialism: "Healing the Wounds of the Past"

M1 NAMIBIA : Herero Demand Reparations From Germany, August 12, 2004

This month marks the 100th anniversary of a German crackdown on an anti-colonial uprising by the Herero ethnic group in Namibia, and descendents of the massacre survivors are demanding reparations and an apology from Germany. In response to an uprising, German soldiers forced the Herero into the desert and cut off access to water sources. Between 45,000 and 65,000 people were killed. Germany now provides more development aid to Namibia than any other country, but the Herero are seeking an official apology and compensation from German companies that profited from the German occupation.

M2 A group of Herero people celebrate Herero day in Okahandja. The day is celebrated on the first Sunday after August 23 every year.

M3 A report from the Deutsche Welle, 11 August 2004

Despite the attempts to overcome the divisions of the past, the *reconciliation* process has been *marred* by a *lawsuit* filed by the Herero People's Reparation Corporation in the US. It seeks $2 billion in damages from several German companies including Deutsche Bank, mining company Terex Corporation and shipping company Deutsche Afrika Linie, all of which *allegedly* profited from Germany's occupation of Namibia.
The German government has refused to consider any compensation claims, pointing to its role as development aid provider in Namibia, as proof of its commitment to *mend fences*.
Earlier this month Germany's Ambassador to Namibia, Wolfgang Massing, said the lawsuit would amount to *naught*. „It will not lead to any results. While it is necessary to remember the past, we should move forward together and find projects that will heal the wounds of the past."

Apology awaited
But the ancestors of the Herero insist on compensation as well as a public apology from Berlin, just as other countries did for the crimes of the Nazi era.

„It was genocide," Herero tribal leader Kuaima Riruako told news agency dpa. „We were massacred and our land, our cattle, our culture was seized." Riruako added that the demand for reparation was an attempt to „restore our dignity and get back what was taken away unfairly from us."
So far German leaders have *skirted* the issue of apologizing to Namibia's ethnic tribes. In January this year, German ambassador Massing regretted the brutal reaction of the German army to the Herero uprising, but refused to react to *allegations* of genocide.
The fact that Germany hasn't officially apologized has angered many in Namibia.
„The Germans have shown themselves as masters of racism, and they lack respect for black people," Arnold Tjihuiko, the chairman of the Herero Committee for memorial festivities, told the newsweekly DER SPIEGEL. „We want the Germans to say, ‚We're sorry!'"

DW staff (sp) http://www.dw-world.de/dw/article/0,,1294643,00.html?mpb=en

---

reconciliation: an end to a disagreement and the start of a good relationship again
to mar: to damage or spoil sth. good
lawsuit: a claim or complaint against sb. that a person or an organization can make in court
allegedly (adv.): to state sth. as a fact but without giving proof
to mend fences: to find a solution to a disagreement with sb.
naught: nothing
to skirt: to avoid talking about a subject, especially because it is difficult or embarrassing
allegation: a public statement that is made without giving proof, accusing sb. of doing sth. that is wrong or illegal

| 1870 | 1875 | 1880 | 1885 | 1890 | 1895 | 1900 | 1905 | 1910 | 1915 | 1920 |

1 Work in groups and prepare a panel discussion on this controversy.
 – Decide which position you want to take.
 – Think of arguments and take notes.
 – Consider counter-arguments.
 – Choose a spokesman and practise your line of argument.
 – Organize a panel discussion in class in which you challenge the other group.

Position:

Arguments:

pro	con

7. New Imperialism and the Scramble for Africa

IV. Africa Today

After 1945 the former colonies gained their independence. Exhausted from their efforts in the Second World War, the European powers were concerned with the process of de-colonization. Some historians say it was too rushed, and resulted in unstable regimes in the newly independent countries, thus causing war in and among them.

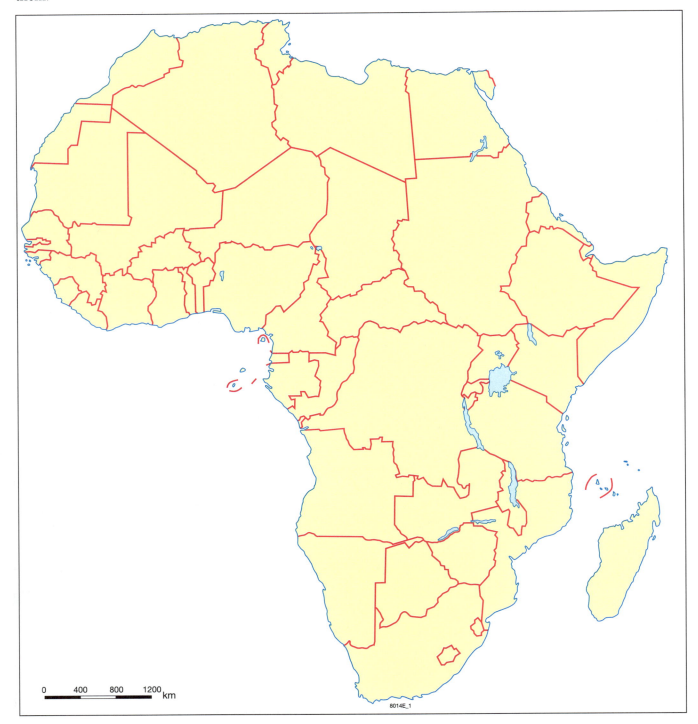

① Find and label the former German colonies *(see textbook, p.114)*.

② Choose one of them and sketch its history from the colonial period until today.
Use the Internet or encyclopaedias.

③ Collect recent news on developments in Africa and discuss them in class.

| 1870 | 1875 | 1880 | 1885 | 1890 | 1895 | 1900 | 1905 | 1910 | 1915 | 1920 |

V. Revision:

1 Important terms to remember: Fill in the missing words using those in the box.

Germany also sought a "place in the sun". Emperor William's policy is known as _____. He engaged Great Britain in a naval race and built up a strong German army. The glorification of armed forces is known as _____. At that time European countries and their peoples were very proud of themselves, and would defend and expand their country whenever necessary or possible. This is known as _____. The _____ of many territories in Africa took place in the late 19th century and sometimes led to the _____ of a whole race or people. The dependencies, or _____, were economically exploited and politically _____.

- colonies
- militarism
- nationalism
- imperialism
- annexation
- genocide
- oppressed

2 Important persons to remember:

Complete the table by adding either the name or the person's importance.

General von Trotha	
	Chancellor of the German Empire from 1900 to 1909 and a strong supporter of German colonialism
Rudyard Kipling	
	German colonist known for his brutal behaviour against the local population in Africa

55

8. The First World War

I. 1914 – the Road to War

M 1 Archduke Franz Ferdinand with Family, about 1910

1 Read the following passage carefully, there are some words missing. Fill in the missing words using the ones in the box.

A fateful day in June

28th June _____ was a warm and sunny day. Archduke Franz Ferdinand of Austria-Hungary and his wife were on an official visit to the town of _____ in the South East of his country. Franz Ferdinand was heir to the _____ throne, which meant that if Emperor Franz Joseph died, then he would be the new Emperor. Sarajevo was in a part of Austria-Hungary where _____ people lived. A lot of them did not like the Austrians and would rather form a country of their own – like Serbia. Some of these people (called _____) wanted to harm the Archduke to show how much they hated Austria-Hungary. One nationalist threw a bomb at the Archduke's car. It did not kill _____ _____ but it made him very angry. He wanted to leave Sarajevo straight away. On the way to the station the Archduke's car stopped when another nationalist was walking by. His name was Gavrilo _____ and he had a gun. He fired at the royal couple and killed them both. This murder (or _____) started a chain of events that led to the Great War.

| Sarajevo | nationalists | Franz Ferdinand | Princip |
| 1914 | Austro-Hungarian | Slav | assassination |

56

II. The Alliances of Europe in 1914

1. Add the names of the major countries.

2. Colour in the countries – one colour for the Entente Powers, one for the Central Powers and one for the neutral countries.

3. Make a legend for your map.

57

8. The First World War

III. Analysing Propaganda

Propaganda is the deliberate spreading of information to make people believe in certain ideas. During the First World War it was used to

– persuade men to volunteer for the army
– keep people confident that the war was being won
– make people hate the enemy so that they would continue the war.

Such material was spread to mass audiences using newspapers, leaflets, posters or films.

M 1 British anti-German poster 1915: Red Cross or Iron Cross?

M 2 A recruiting poster released by the British government in 1915: Women of Britain say "Go!"

① Describe the posters and the feelings they are trying to arouse in the public.

| 1910 | 1911 | 1912 | 1913 | 1914 | 1915 | 1916 | 1917 | 1918 | 1919 | 1920 |

2 Which of the two posters do you think is more effective in encouraging people to fight? Discuss the reasons with your partner.

3 An American senator said in 1917 that "The first casualty when war comes is the truth". What do you think he meant? Do you agree or disagree?

8. The First World War

IV. Working with statistics

Statistics can be presented in many different ways. Graphs and charts can show development or help to compare conditions *(see textbook, p. 71, "Analysing Statistics")*.

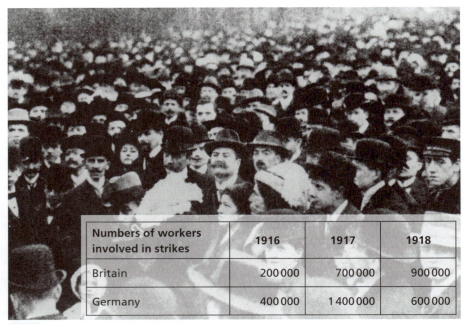

Numbers of workers involved in strikes	1916	1917	1918
Britain	200 000	700 000	900 000
Germany	400 000	1 400 000	600 000

M 1 A Strike in Germany, 1917

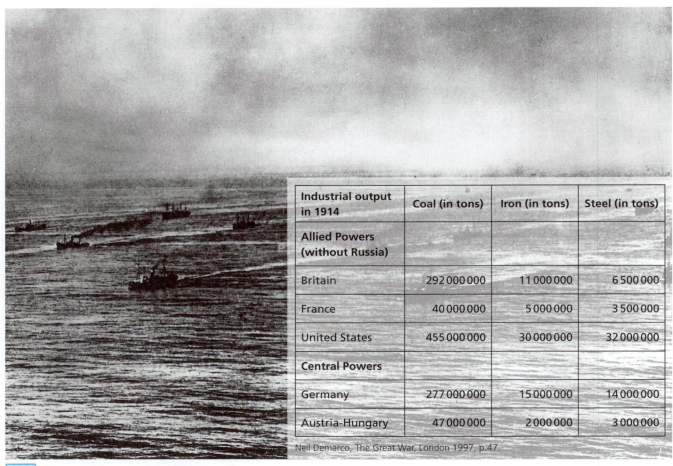

Industrial output in 1914	Coal (in tons)	Iron (in tons)	Steel (in tons)
Allied Powers (without Russia)			
Britain	292 000 000	11 000 000	6 500 000
France	40 000 000	5 000 000	3 500 000
United States	455 000 000	30 000 000	32 000 000
Central Powers			
Germany	277 000 000	15 000 000	14 000 000
Austria-Hungary	47 000 000	2 000 000	3 000 000

Neil Demarco, The Great War, London 1997, p. 47.

M 2 Convoy in the First World War, 1917

| 1910 | 1911 | 1912 | 1913 | 1914 | 1915 | 1916 | 1917 | 1918 | 1919 | 1920 |

1 Does M1 suggest that strikes were an important factor in causing Germany's defeat?

_____

_____

_____

_____

_____

_____

2 What does M2 suggest about the impact of America's entry into the war?

_____

_____

_____

_____

_____

_____

3 Make a bar chart to compare the steel production of the different powers in 1914.

14078E_1

61

8. The First World War

V. Revision

M 1 Battleground at Verdun, 1918

1 Ten important terms to remember: Find them.

sailors refuse to obey the orders of their officers	
getting an army ready to fight in a war	
long deep holes in the ground to protect soldiers	
stopping goods from entering or leaving a country	
new weapon of war making the US enter the war	
time of hunger in Germany 1916/17	
name for a year of great changes (1917)	
agreement to stop fighting	
a situation in which no progress can be made	
famous battle symbolizing the war of attrition	

2 Dates: What happened? Complete the table.

28 June 1914	
April 1917	
October 1917	
March 1918	

62

3) Persons: Write in one or two sentences why these people were important for the history of the First World War.

M 2 Alfred Graf von Schlieffen (1833–1913)

M 3 Woodrow Wilson (1856–1924)

M 4 Vladimir Ilyich Lenin (1870–1924)

M 5 Paul von Hindenburg (1847–1934)

Picture Credits

akg-images, Berlin:
Schutzumschlag, 8, 10, 11 o. + Mi., 12 o.li. + u.,
13 u., 20, 21, 30, 56, 62, 63 o. (2) + u.re.
Anstey, D.: 18/19

Bildarchiv Preußischer Kulturbesitz, Berlin:
11 u., 13 Mi.re., 22, 23 li. (2) + re. (Freies
Deutsches Hochstift, Frankfurt/M.), 27 o.li.,
40 o., 44, 48 (L. Braun), 50 (SBB/D. Katz)
Bismarck Museum, Friedrichsruh:
40 u. (Carstensen, Hamburg)
Bridgeman Art Library: 16/17
(Private Collection/Roger-Viollet)

CORBIS, Düsseldorf: 13 o.re. (B. Burkhardt)

Das Fotoarchiv, Essen: 12 o.re. (M. Dlouhy)
Deutsches Museum, München: 25 (2)

Historisches Museum der Stadt Wien: 34

Klöckner, J., Köln: 6

Langner, P., Hannover: 32

Museum of the City of New York: 28 re.

Picture Alliance, Frankfurt/M.:
13 Mi.li. (Helga Lade Fotoagentur/R. Binder),
52 (dpa/J. Schmitt)

Staatliche Kunsthalle, Karlsruhe: 38 o.
SV Bilderdienst, München: 13 o.li. (KPA)

Tonn, D., Bovenden: 5, 7

ullstein bild, Berlin:
14 o. (Granger Collection), 35 (Archiv
Gerstenberg), 60 o. + u., 63 u.li. (Imago)
© Universitätsbibliothek, Heidelberg:
38 Mi. (KLA_1848_111)

alle übrigen Schaubilder und Karten:
Westermann Kartographie/Technisch
Graphische Abteilung, Braunschweig